DEAR SANTA

DEAR SANTA

CHILDREN'S CHRISTMAS
LETTERS AND WISH LISTS,
1870-1920

LETTERS SELECTED BY
MARY HARRELL-SESNIAK

COMMENTARY BY
J. HARMON FLAGSTONE

CHRONICLE BOOKS
SAN FRANCISCO

Library of Congress Cataloging-in-Publication Data available.

ISBN 978-1-4521-4018-6

Manufactured in China

Design by Ryan Hayes

10 9 8 7 6 5 4 3 2 1

Chronicle Books LLC
680 Second Street
San Francisco, California 94107
www.chroniclebooks.com

CONTENTS

THE
HISTORY
OF THE
SANTA LETTER

"Yes, Virginia, there is a Santa Claus." These famous words, now a beloved fixture in our Christmas tradition, originally appeared in editor Frank Church's letter to an eight-year-old New Yorker named Virginia O'Hanlon. The letter was printed in New York's *The Sun* on September 21, 1897, in an effort to reassure Virginia of Santa's existence. The young lady, whose friends were skeptical about his existence, wanted to know if Santa was real. Virginia's father told her to ask the newspaper because "If you see it in *The Sun*, it's so." Church's reply, published for the nation to see, charmed readers and galvanized the American Santa tradition—a tradition that newspapers played no small role in establishing. All the letters in this book originally appeared in newspapers, often having been routed there by postal workers who didn't know what else to do with them. Newspapers typeset and published the letters, retaining all the charming idiosyncrasies of the handwritten letters, including typos, misspellings, and endearing grammatical errors. (We, too, have retained those idiosyncrasies in the selections that appear in this book.) Among many other joys these letters brought to audiences, newspaper publication of Santa letters invited adults to reconnect with their childhood. This book, containing more than 125 fascinating letters from 1870 to 1920, invites you to do the same—to rediscover the Christmas spirit and the magical possibilities of the holiday season by seeing it through the eyes of a child.

Continuing the great tradition, children from around the world still write letters to Santa. In America, the ritual went mainstream in the second half of the nineteenth century, due in part to a cartoon by Thomas Nast that included Santa's fictional address: "Santa Claussville, N.P." (short for North Pole). Children began addressing letters to that address and mailed them through the United States Postal Service. For years, they were redirected to the dead letter office, unread and undeliverable. Then, in 1912, Postmaster General Frank Hitchcock authorized postal employees and volunteer citizens to respond to the letters in order to ensure that every American child's holiday wish might come true. By the end of World War II, "Operation Santa" had become a cultural institution, making its Hollywood debut in the famous courtroom climax of *Miracle on 34th Street* (1947), in which postal workers toss mountainous piles of letters before the bench of Judge Henry X. Harper as indisputable proof of Kris Kringle's identity as the real Santa.

Indeed, Santa Claus receives more mail than any other figure in the world—an average of more than five million letters per year—due in part to the participation of postal services who maintain a working relationship with Santa. American children can send letters to Mr. Claus, 4141 Postmark Drive, Anchorage, Alaska 99530-9998. English children can mail them to Santa's Grotto in Reindeerland, XM4 5HQ. Canadian children can mail them to Santa Claus, North Pole, Canada, H0H 0H0 (a postal code that, in letters and numbers, mirrors Santa's jolly laugh, "Ho, ho, ho!"). Children of any nationality can send letters directly to the Santa Claus Main Post Office in Rovaniemi, Finland—located precisely at the Arctic Circle—which has received nearly twenty million letters from around the world since 1985.

Prior to the global implementation of the modern postal system in the late 1800s, children around the world relied on a variety of methods to deliver messages to Santa Claus, many of which are still employed today. In England, for example, children placed their letters in the fireplace, where their wishes were magically turned to smoke and drifted through the sky toward Santa's wintry kingdom in the North Pole. Scottish children would "cry up the lum" by sticking their heads up the chimney and shouting their Christmas wishes out loud for Santa to hear. Throughout Europe, the tradition was to leave a letter in one's shoe beside the chimney or the Christmas tree where Santa would be sure to see it. Swiss children would awaken to find a piece of chocolate on the windowsill, left by Santa as a confirmation of receipt. Latin American children attach their letters to balloons and loft them heavenward in hopes that they will reach Santa. In the United States, Canada, and Australia, children leave their letters on the kitchen table, or by the Christmas tree or fireside, alongside a plate of cookies and a glass of milk (for Santa) and generous clusters of carrots (for Santa's reindeer).

These days, children can launch their messages into the electronic ether of cyberspace. Santa now welcomes e-mail messages and video messages sent on the Internet. However, despite the dominance of new media technology in our everyday lives, the handwritten Santa letter tradition continues to thrive: the volume of Santa's "snail mail" correspondence grows every year, and far exceeds the number of yearly e-mail messages in his Arctic inbox.

Writing letters to Santa is more than just an opportunity for children to pour forth their hearts' desires to an attentive ear. It's also an exercise in literary expression, often being a child's very first attempt at letter writing. In addition, it offers a sentimental education for the human heart. Witness the selfless compassion of one kindhearted Australian girl (page 161) who pleaded with Santa in 1916 to "give an extra gift or two to the poor little

Belgian and Servian boys and girls who have suffered so much." Santa letters also offer a window into the changing times—the historical events and material objects, particularly toys, that shape the culture of an era.

Above all, the letters reflect the immortal hope of the child in all of us. Today, more than ever, the famous words of Francis Church ring true. "No Santa Claus!" he replied to Virginia in disbelief that any should doubt Santa's existence. "Thank God! He lives, and he lives forever. A thousand years from now, Virginia, nay, ten times ten thousand years from now, he will continue to make glad the heart of childhood." *Dear Santa* is the story of childhood, told in letters that express the oldest, best, and most ardent wishes of the human spirit—letters that gladden the hearts of children of all ages.

INTRODUCTION

THE

ORIGINS

OF

SANTA CLAUS

O nce upon a time, there lived a man with three daughters. The man's poverty prevented him from giving his daughters a marriage dowry, and without husbands they were sure to be sold into slavery. One evening, a good man named Nicholas—who was known to have devoted his life to helping those in need—dropped a bag of gold down the man's chimney, enough to enable the oldest daughter to marry. The next night, another bag of gold came tumbling down the chimney, enough to allow the man's second daughter to marry. On the third night, when the final bag arrived, the father was waiting for Nicholas. The father begged Nicholas to accept a gift in return for his generosity. Nicholas refused everything that was offered him, and instead praised God as the true source of the father's good fortune.

This legend is the most famous story surrounding the origin of the Santa Claus we know today. The real Saint Nicholas lived in the fourth century in the region we now know as Turkey, where he was the bishop of a town called Myra. Born into a wealthy family, he donated his entire inheritance to the poor people of his native city, leaving a legacy of selfless gift giving that informed the evolution of our modern Santa tradition. Families in ancient Europe and Asia Minor celebrated St. Nicholas' Day on December 6—the anniversary of his death—with an annual feast, during which children would leave food for St. Nicholas and straw for his donkey and discover toys and sweets in their place the next morning.

One of the most popular saints in Renaissance Europe, St. Nicholas became the prototype for a variety of gift-giving figures throughout the world. In Germany, Austria, and neighboring countries, the Santa-like figure is an angelic child named the *Christkind* or *Chriskindl* (Christ child), from which the American nickname "Kris Kringle" is derived. In England, it is Father Christmas who fills stockings with holiday treats. His French counterpart, who fills children's shoes, is known as Père Noël. In Italy, a benevolent old witch named La Befana floats down chimneys on her magic broomstick, delivering toys to well-behaved children. *Ded Moroz* (Father Frost) travels across the vast land of Russia with his granddaughter, the Snowmaiden, on a sleigh pulled by three powerful Russian stallions, delivering gifts to Russian children on New Year's Eve rather than Christmas Eve. In Brazil, where Christmas arrives in the hot summertime and where most homes do not have fireplaces, Papai Noel wears an airy, silken Santa suit and delivers his gifts through the front door.

The American Santa Claus tradition originated with the Dutch colonists in the seventeenth century settlement of New Amsterdam (now New York City). Elsewhere in the American colonies, Puritan settlers who repudiated the veneration of the Catholic canon of saints discouraged the tradition. They prohibited any mention of St. Nicholas's name, as well as the associated traditions of caroling, gift giving, and candle lighting. But the Dutch colonists celebrated Saint Nicholas and the Christmas holidays with merriment. In fact, the American nickname "Santa Claus" evolved from St. Nicholas's Dutch nickname, Sinterklaas.

At the beginning of the nineteenth century, the New York Historical Society named Saint Nicholas as their patron saint in honor of the city's Dutch heritage. Among the members of the society was writer Washington Irving, best known for his stories "Rip Van Winkle" and "The Legend of Sleepy Hollow." It was Washington Irving who created the first narrative sketch of the Saint Nicholas (or Sinterklaas) figure, describing him in his satirical *A History of New York* (1809) as a pipe-smoking, broad-hatted Dutchman often seen "riding over the tops of the trees, in that self-same wagon wherein he brings his yearly presents to children."

But fellow society member Clement Clarke Moore left an even greater mark on our Christmas tradition. In 1823, his poem "The Night Before Christmas" (originally published as "A Visit from St. Nicholas") appeared in the *Troy Sentinel* newspaper. Moore's Santa is more elfin than human. He is diminutive, plump and jolly, and laden with toys. He descends chimneys, fills stockings, and pilots a flying sleigh led by "eight tiny rein-deer"—all original creations of Moore's poetic fancy. Moore's poem also moved Santa's annual journey from St. Nicholas' Eve (which, at the time, was celebrated on December 5) to December 24, or Christmas Eve.

But it is illustrator Thomas Nast—known as the "Father of the American Cartoon"—who is credited with inventing many of Santa's most iconic traits. In a series of portraits and illustrations for *Harper's Weekly* from 1863 to 1886, he depicted Santa as a jolly, bearded man—no longer an elf, as Moore had envisioned him—in a red, fur-trimmed suit. Nast's Santa lived at the North Pole, carried a toy-filled sack, made "naughty or nice" lists, and had the addresses of every little boy and girl in the world.

The realism of Nast's work set a precedent for Santa illustrations of the ensuing century. Santa became more human-looking, and his surroundings became more modern. As the new century progressed, Santa's reindeer were often aided by more advanced methods of transportation—steamships, railways, and airplanes, for example—and the North Pole's elf-managed production facilities became mechanized and automated. Santa even got married! In 1899, Kathy Bates, author of the Christmas tale *Goody Santa Claus on a Sleigh Ride*, created Mrs. Claus, a charming domestic companion for the Arctic's most eligible bachelor.

The tradition of visiting the "real" Santa at department stores began one afternoon in 1890 when James Edgar, proprietor of the Boston Store in Brockton, Massachusetts, wore a Santa suit to the store. Over the next few months, Edgar's new marketing strategy became so popular that people traveled from as far as Rhode Island just to get a glimpse of him. By the 1920s, department store Santas had become a staple of American consumer culture, so much so that in 1937, longtime Santa impersonator Charles W. Howard—also the star of the Macy's Thanksgiving Day Parade from 1948 to 1965—opened the nation's first Santa school, which taught the various fine arts of Santa Claus impersonation. And, in 1947, the Oscar-winning film *Miracle on 34th Street* hit theaters, offering a unique glimpse of this beloved Christmas tradition.

By the beginning of the twentieth century, Santa had also become a star of America's booming advertising industry. His 1903 portfolio included Shredded Wheat, Pear's Soap, and

Waterman's Fountain Pens. In 1931, the Coca-Cola Company commissioned artist Haddon Sundblom to paint Santa for an ad campaign. Sundblom's version of Santa was jolly, rotund, and larger than life, and featured the merry face now instantly recognizable worldwide. The image rapidly spread across America on billboards, in magazines and newspapers, and on Coke products. This advertising campaign helped standardize the modern image of Santa Claus.

Though Santa's face and form have changed throughout the centuries—from his saintly origins, to his elfin and human representations in popular literature and art, and finally to his contemporary status as a global pop-cultural icon—his spirit has remained the same, transcending historical and national affiliations. An example of selfless sharing and unconditional love, he is a powerful role model, an embodiment of human generosity, and a source of joy to the young—and young at heart—around the world.

LETTERS

1870

1879

THE
1870s

The 1870s was a decade of invention and discovery. The British Empire was the era's dominant political power, and its imperial ambition was felt throughout the world. In America, the decade was defined by the nation's effort to rebuild itself following the Civil War. During this time, Alexander Graham Bell developed the prototype of the modern telephone and Thomas Edison produced the world's first working phonograph and first functional lightbulb; while the French Impressionists, such as Claude Monet and Jean Renoir, revolutionized the art of painting. Christmas became a symbol of national healing in the wake of the war, and Congress declared Christmas a federal holiday in 1870. Christmas also became big business. Department stores like Macy's stocked toys from all over the world. The standardization of the postal delivery system in the years following the Civil War made the sending of Christmas cards to friends and relatives across the vast nation a new American pastime—and gave children confidence that their letters would reach Santa Claus.

LETTER HIGHLIGHTS
OF THE 1870S

TOY TERMINOLOGY

- A toy *buggy*, like the one requested by Maggie in Canton, Ohio (page 26), is a doll carriage.
- The *case* that Little Julia of Springfield, Illinois (page 28), requested for her hymn and prayer book would likely have been leather, and might have featured a leather strap for carrying the books like a small purse.
- Little Julia also requested *Arctic overshoes*, alluding to a popular theme in the American cultural imagination of the second half of the nineteenth century—arctic exploration and life at the North Pole. These overshoes would have protected her indoor shoes from harsh Illinois winter weather.
- *The Bodley Books*, requested by William from Wilmington, North Carolina (page 29), were a popular series of children's books written by Bostonian Horace Scudder in the second half of the nineteenth century.
- On behalf of his sister, William also requested a *jump-jack*, referring to a Jumping Jack, a popular Victorian toy with a string that, when pulled, caused the jester's arms and legs to move.

- Another of William's requests was *stick of pomade* for his father, which was a popular oil-based hair-grooming aid for men of the Victorian era.

THE CHARM OF CHILDREN

The letter writers of this decade evince a touching concern with Santa's mode of arrival. Maggie (page 24) offers to hang her stocking outside the door so Santa won't have to come down the "dirty" chimney. Louie (page 26), concerned about the small size of his family's chimney, suggests to Santa that he enter through the roomier trapdoor. Howard (page 30) assures Santa that his reindeer will have a safe landing on his "low" rooftop.

LIVING HISTORY

The Soldiers' Children's Home mentioned in the letter of Alice from Trenton, New Jersey (page 25), was a living facility in New Jersey offered to the children of soldiers who had died in the Civil War, which claimed more than six hundred thousand lives. This home was one of many around the nation that were supported by the government and donations from citizens in the decades following the war.

- *Anna's sincerity.* Anna of Chicago, Illinois (page 27), aware that hard times have befallen her family and concerned that her siblings might not get any gifts, implores Santa to pay them a visit. For herself, she asks for a doll—but only if Santa has one to spare: "If you have any dolls left, bring one to me and I will be so glad."

- *Dickie's proactive approach.* Putting his best foot forward, Dickie of Boston, Massachusetts (page 31), opens his letter by identifying himself as a "bright-eyed little boy" who has been "trying to be good." He then goes on to share his holiday wish list. And to preempt any harsh judgment from Santa, he confesses that he might have over-reached: "I hope you will not think I am asking for too many things, for I do not wish to be thought greedy."

- *Cora's Christmas spirit.* In a selfless gesture, Cora of Green Ridge, Missouri (page 32), concludes her letter by reminding Santa not to overlook those less fortunate than herself: "Now, dear Santa Claus, please don't forget any of the poor little children this time."

1870

HILLSBORO, OHIO

Dear Santa Claus,

I never hung up my stocking, because I didn't know. Will you excuse it? Please don't forget to come here this time. I will hang it on the outside of the door, and grandma's too. So you won't have to come down the chimney. It's very dirty. And I won't peep. You'll know grandma's, because it is blue.

Good-by,

Maggie

1871

Dear Santa;

There is a little girl in the Soldiers' Children's Home, and she thinks she needs a writing desk. Having heard that your heart grows very large about Christmas time, I write this letter to ask you to be kind enough to favor this little Alice with the article she desires. I am that little girl, and promise you that I will try to improve in writing if you grant my request.

Yours in hope.

Alice

1874
CANTON, OHIO

Dear Santa Claus:

We have moved. We don't live where we used to. We moved our shop to East Tuscarawas street, in Cassilly's frame building. Our chimney is small, but we have a trap door, and you can come down easy.

Louie

1874
CANTON, OHIO

Dear Santa Claus:

We moved in Patton's house, North Market street, and I wish you would send me a doll and a little buggy and sleigh; our chimney is big enough to come down. Do send my little cousin Fannie a buggy too; be sure and come. I will be a good little girl.

Maggie

26

1876

CHICAGO, ILLINOIS

Mr Santa Claus.

Mama says that papa has been out of work so
long that you will forget to come to our house,
but Willie & Ruth will feel so bad that I thout
I would write to tell you to come if you could.
I am glad I learned to write at school, for if I
had not I would not know how to get word to
you we live on Ambrose Street, and my name
is Anna.

if you have any dolls left bring one to me and
I will be so glad

Anna

I forgot to tell you that papa cant get any work
and mama feels real bad because the money
is most all gone and the babys shoes are worn
out, wish I knew some of your little girls so I
could see all the play things it would be so nice

I could not find any other envelop

1876

Dear Santa Claus:

I thought I would write to you about my presents. I want a little prayer-book; I go to the Episcopal church. I would like to have a pair of Arctic overshoes, and I want a pair of buttoned shoes. We are going to have a Christmas tree at our Sunday-school. Please bring me some candy and whatever you have that you think I would like. I am making a little present for my papa. I would like to have a hymn with my prayer-book in a little case. Good-by: come a week from to-night: come on West Monroe street, and you will find the stocking of

Little Julia.

1878

WILMINGTON, NORTH CAROLINA

Dear Santa Claus:

Please bring me a village and the third volume of the Bodley Books, and please bring Annie a trunk and a book, jumping-rope and a jump-jack, and please bring Imogene a book and a jumping-rope. Please bring mamma one of the following things: Two small frames, a pair of blankets, writing-paper, a new frame for oil-painting, or anything else, and papa a stick of pomade. We are trying to be good, and I hope I have not asked for too much. We all send love.

Your affectionate friend,

William

1878

CARTERSVILLE, GEORGIA

Dear Mr. Santa Clause:

I'm bothering you again, as Christmas is here.
Well to begin with, I want some fine paper and
envelopes, and a finger ring and something
else nice. Please leave a little note as to how
you are getting on—also your family. Good bye,
Santa Clause. I wish you well until next year.
Please put a little something in my stocking.
Our house is low and you can easily get on it
with your reindeer. Our house is three miles
from the village of Cartersville. I have been in
Washington, but am at home now. I hope you
can find me. Good bye, dear Santa Clause.

Howard

1878

Mr. Santa Claus,

I am a bright-eyed little boy, and am trying to be good so that you will remember me on Christmas morning. I would very much like to have a bayonet, a gun, a sword, a sled, a watch and a chain, a pair of rubber boots, a snow shovel, some books, a slate, some nice warm stockings, a little pen-knife, a candy cane and a pair of mittens. I hope you will not think I am asking for too many things, for I do not wish to be thought greedy. Mamma sends love, and hopes you will remember her too.

Dickie

1878

Dear Santa C'aus:

I want a large Doll, with blue eyes and a set of Dishes and some candy and peanuts and a pair of gloves. Now, dear Santa Claus, please don't forget any of the poor little children this time. Good-bye.

Cora

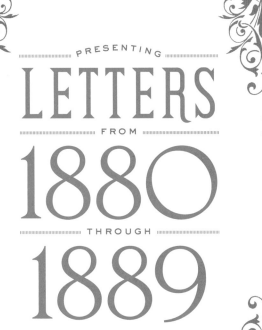

PRESENTING

LETTERS

FROM

1880

THROUGH

1889

THE
1880s

The 1880s were a period of economic prosperity and imperial ambition for the modern European nations. Rising powers such as Germany, France, and Spain vied with the British Empire for global influence, while America was experiencing the Gilded Age, an era of robust capitalism. In the arts, literary fiction flourished, and the decade saw the creation of such legendary characters as Sir Arthur Conan Doyle's Sherlock Holmes, Robert Louis Stevenson's Dr. Jekyll, and Mark Twain's Huckleberry Finn. Industrial developments of the decade ranged from the world's first skyscraper to the world's first motion picture camera. Symbolizing America's aspiring ambitions of the age, the Brooklyn Bridge was completed in 1883, and the Statue of Liberty opened in New York Harbor in 1886. Prompted by the surge of the economy and the rise of mass production, Christmas gift giving flourished on a grand scale in the 1880s, much to the delight of the children of this decade, whose wish lists grew even more colorful and elaborate—indeed, as ambitious as the decade itself.

LETTER HIGHLIGHTS OF THE 1880S

- A *velocipede*, requested by Clyde of Lawrence, Kansas (page 38), is a vehicle with one or more wheels that is powered by human effort, such as a unicycle, bicycle, or tricycle.
- *Gaiters*, requested by a child from Lexington, Missouri (page 46), are protective covering garments worn over the shoe or the lower part of the leg.
- A *french harp*, requested by Eddie from Springfield, Ohio (page 54), is a harmonica.
- A *box of sealing wax*, requested by Edith in Harrisburg, Pennsylvania (page 47), would have been used for sealing letters, an old-fashioned method preferred by some to the gummed envelopes that were gaining popularity during this decade.
- A *coaster*, also requested by Edith, likely refers to a snow sled.
- Minnie of Chicago, Illinois (page 55), requests a *hooking ladder* on behalf of her brother, referring to a "hook and ladder" set, an ancestor of the modern-day fire truck. This toy would have been made of cast iron and would have been pulled by a pair of toy horses.

As the letters of this decade attest, dolls, dollhouses, and doll accessory items were popular Christmas gifts in the 1880s. Katie (page 41) wants a little doll buggy, a tea set, a bedroom set, a little stove, and a parlor set. Mina (page 42), who already has a doll and "so [has] no need of one," requests a beautiful furnished dollhouse with a dining table, kitchen set and tea set, and a doll fan. Charley's sister Eva (page 52) wants a "little trunk to keep her doll in." Edith (page 47), too, wants a "doll's trunk."

THE CHARM OF CHILDREN

The heartfelt generosity of Laurinda and Edwin from Fort Wayne, Indiana (page 57), is reflected in their altruistic sentiments. The siblings want to "buy things for poor little children who have no mama and papa" because they "want others to be happy."

LIVING HISTORY

Charley and Eva (page 52) refer to having seen President Grover Cleveland when he passed through their hometown. This stop would have been part of the president's national goodwill tour of 1887. The president, who before then had rarely traveled outside of New York State, decided to tour America in a specially designed deluxe Pullman train car to enhance his political visibility and national popularity. The spectacle had its intended effect on Charley, who wants "to be President of the United States" when he grows up.

DID YOU KNOW . . . ?

The character of Santa's wife did not officially become part of American holiday mythology until 1889 when Katherine Lee Bates popularized Mrs. Claus in her book *Goody Santa Claus on a Sleigh Ride*. Edith's postscript (page 47), "P.S. How's your wife?", and a request from Little Pearl of Wellington, Kansas (page 49)—"I would like to see your wife, I love her too"—both invoke Santa's better half, attesting to the growing curiosity in Mrs. Claus in the years leading up to the book's publication.

DON'T MISS . . .

• *Arthur's shyness.* Arthur, of Chicago, Illinois (page 56), requests a present for a "little poor boy" he knows who "stays all alone" during the day while his mother works. It is not until the final line of his letter that we discover that the "little poor boy" is actually Arthur himself.

1880

LAWRENCE, KANSAS

Good Santa Clause:

I wish you would bring me a velocipede and some other toys and a pair of skates.

Yours truly,

Clyde

1880

LAWRENCE, KANSAS

Dear Santa Clause:

Will you please bring me a box of handkerchiefs and a little doll about three inches long.

Yours truly,

Josie

1880

ROCKPORT, KENTUCKY

Dear Santa Claus:

I send you this letter to let you know what I want. I want a pistol and some caps and some fire-crackers and some candy; and Santa, do not forget me; bring me two boxes of candies.

Your little friend,

Frankie

1881

NASHVILLE, TENNESSEE

Dear Santa Claus:

I wish you would bring me a big doll and a little doll buggy. I am a little girl, five years old, and I would like to have a tea set, a bed room set, a little stove and a parlor set. I will not ask for much this Christmas, dear Santa Claus, for you brought me so many things last Christmas. Please bring me a little doll, piano and Chinese baby—I think they are so nice. Well, you must excuse me for not writing a long letter. I expect you will receive a great many letters from little girls. I remain yours.

Katie

1882

Dear Santa Claus:

I am a little girl eight years old. Please bring me a doll house, furnished, and a dining table. I have a beautiful doll, so have no need of one. Please bring me a kitchen set, and a tea set, and a few pretty pictures, and a fairy tale book. I have got everything that you brought me last Christmas. I wish you a happy Christmas. Please sir bring me a doll fan. My little brother was so pleased when he saw the snow to-day that if we would ask him who sent it he would say that Santa Claus did. I live on South Trade street. I never knew exactly where to direct your letters before I saw your card in the Observer. I send my love to you.

Yours affectionate,

Mina.

1883

Dear Old Santa Claus:

I call you old, because Papa says, you are the same "Santa Claus" that lived when Grand Pa was a little boy, and he is over 75 years old now. Papa says you are either at the North Pole, or in Norway or Russia today, he don't know exactly where, but if I write you through the *Watchman and Southron* you will be sure to get my letter, as it is a very popular paper and goes everywhere.

Dear Santa, please come and see us once more next Monday night. Papa says times are so hard and money so scarce, that he is afraid you won't be able to come, and make us have a "Merry and Happy Christmas."

You mustn't buy and bring us expensive presents, but only some little trifle to make our hearts glad.

I am going to be very good because Mama says you never go to see bad little girls. I am going to hang up a stocking for myself and for each of my little sisters, I have two you know, and I think I will also hang up one for our nurse, and also for the little boy that brings us our meals; there is also a nice little boy in our house, one of our little cousins, he plays so nicely with us, just like a little girl, has dolls, and sews, and if he wore a dress instead of pants, and jacket he would pass for a little girl. I think I will hang up a stocking for him too—we are all going to bed early, because mama says you won't come until we are asleep, and I do wan't you to come "so bad." If you don't I will be disappointed, I'll cry. Don't forget Sumter next Monday night, but come and make all our little hearts glad—I have some nice little cousins in the house around the corner, and they are all anxiously looking for you. Good bye until next Monday night.

One of your many little expectant friends

1884

Dear Santey Closse:

My father is dead and my mother is poor and I want a new pair of shose and stokings and a gosmer and umbrella and tooth brush. My mother says will you please bring her pair shoes for Sunday and a pair stokings for Christmas I close my letter

Maggie

1884

My Friend Santa Claus:

I thought I would write to you and let you know what I want for Christmas, so now I will tell you, I want a pair of rubber shoes, and a pair of gloves, and a sled, and a book, and a pair of garters, and some candy, and some almonds, and some oranges, and some lemons. And Ma wants a handsome cashmere dress, and a three dollars pair of gaiters, and a handsome new market cloak, and a fifteen or twenty dollars for pocket money, and a bolt of good canton flannel. And Pa wants a thousand dollars pocket money. And my sister wants a nice cash-mere dress trimed with velvet, and two or three nice stories books. and a nice pair of over-shoes, and a nice pair of kid gaiters, and some candy, and a orange, and a lemon and any thing else you choose to bring her. Thats all.

1885

Dear Santa Claus:

I must tell you just where I live. I live across the Atlantic Ocean, in North America, in the United States, below the Dominion of Canada, in Pennsylvania, in the city of Harrisburg. I am sorry that I must write so much just to tell you where I live, and now I have forgotten to tell you what street I live on and what number. I live on the south part of Second street. I must tell you what I want too. Well, first I want a doll with long, golden, curly hair like Florence, or if you cannot get one like that will you try and get a nice lovely one? The second thing is a doll's trunk, and the third thing is a box of sealing wax. I guess I can have five things and next, if I can have two more things, I want a big coaster like Mame, and then I want a bank that is down in the same block as I live in, only down next to the corner it represents a roller staking rink and that is all I have to say, Good bye,

Edith

P.S. How's your wife? Answer.

47

1885

WASHINGTON, DISTRICT OF COLUMBIA

FROM A PAIR OF FRIENDS

Dear santa clauss—

I want a beautiful french doll that will talk and a tricycle and a dear little sister and a dear little baby of my own.

Rosita

Dear Santa Claus—

Please bring me a little sister, a dear little puppie. Please let Rosita live together next door to ourfamily.

Josephine

1885

WELLINGTON, KANSAS

Dear Old Santa Claus

I never loved you as well as I do now I have been reading a bout you in the eagle and your headquarters in wichita.

And fore fear you wont come to wellington, I will tell you what I want you to bring me christmas.

a doll and buggy and a fairy book, and a parlor set for dolly and lots of canndy and bon-bons.

I would like to see your wife, I love her too, and your little elves at works on those pretty things.

I am a little girl, and cant write very well, am only seven years old, But I hope you can read this

I am so sleepy, please dont forget.

little Pearl

1885

FROM A BROTHER AND SISTER

You look so kind and pleasant in pictures, that I thought maybe you would send me a nice lace collar for a Christmas present if I would write you a short letter and tell you that I wanted one.

I send this to Washington because it is the capital of our country and I think you live there. I wish I could see the place just once and I would be happy.

P.S. I have been told there was not any Santa, but I don't believe it.

Will you please be so kind as to send me a pair of skates? I am nine years of age and wear a number one shoe.

P.X. I do not know where you live; but I suppose you live in Washington, for it is the capital of the United States.

50

1887
LAWRENCE, KANSAS

Dear Santa Claus:

When you bring the toys won't you please stop at Luther's and bring me two sweet oranges, some mixed nuts, a few eating apples, a box of holiday biscuits, a few nice raisins and just *lots* of candy. And if it won't be too big a load mamma would like a whole basketful of groceries, and a big turkey.

I am so sleepy I guess this will do for this time, so good-night.

Yours,

Gertie

1887

Dear Santa Claus:

I will write and tell you what I hope you will give me and little sister Eva I want a Round Runner Sled so I can go a coasting every day and a good Pocket Knife I would like a pair of shoes to if you dont forget me I am 12 years old and am in 3d Reader I love to go to school Mr Santa Claus I want to be President of the United States when I am a man so Every one will want to see me like they did Mr. Cleveland when he came to Kansas City this summer. My mother is a poor widow but she is good to me and I love her. When I get to be a big man I will work hard for ma. Santa Claus, little sister wants a little trunk to keep her doll in and you can put some candy in the trunk, for she loves candy. If I give her one cent she buys candy for it. She is 10 years old, and, Dear Santa Claus, we had just the cutest little Baby girl left at our doorstep last April. Ma kept her and named her Nelley. She is so good and we all love her so very much. She can say da-da.

I don't Know what you can Bring to her. I guess you Know now. I hope you won't get Angry at me for writing you such a long letter. I would like to get a letter from you. Well Santa good by. Oh I live at Main st., Kan. City Mo.

Dear Santa claus, pleas dont forget us as you did last year. Love to you.

Charley and Eva

1887

SPRINGFIELD, OHIO

Dear Santa Claus—

I would like to have a nice pair of mittens and a french harp.

Eddie

1888

Dear Santa Claws:

Do not forget us six Children Minnie Asher Eddie Martha Emma and Harry

Asher 3 years wants a slay and a waggon with express on it and a drum engine and hooking ladder.

Eddie 13 years wants a fute and a drum.

Martha 7 years wants a buggie and a doll and set of dishes.

Emma She is 9 years old and wants a little set of dishes and a buggie.

Harry is 5 years old he wants a drum and a fife.

I want a piano, a table a big doll and set of dishes.

Minnie

1888

CHICAGO, ILLINOIS

Dear Santa Claws:

There is a little poor boy that lives on Ada St. He stays all alone while his mother works. I told him I would ask Santa Claws to bring him a rocking horse. his name is Arthur. He is a good little boy. He lives on ada st. highest flat.

This is writ by Arthur

1888

FORT WAYNE, INDIANA

Dear, Good Santa Claus:

Brother and I send you fifty cents (50c) to help buy things for poor little children who have no papa and mamma. We are happy ourselves and we want others to be happy. We wish you and everybody a merry Christmas.

Laurinda and Edwin

1888

Good Morning Dear Santa—

We are two little children and we thought we would send our names and we have with us a little orphan child only 6 years old. He got no mama, no papa. So Santa Claus won't you come down our chimney, please sir. So good-bye Mr. Santa. Don't forget us, Papa is sick now. Mama is not well. Sister can't give us no Christmas.

PRESENTING

LETTERS

FROM

1890

THROUGH

1899

In the 1890s, while the European powers expanded their territories abroad through colonial conquest, significant portions of their domestic populations moved to America. In 1892, the flood of immigration prompted the federal government to open up Ellis Island in New York Harbor. Millions of immigrants would pass through its doors in the ensuing decades, becoming Americans in the process. Symbolizing its coming of age on the world stage, America hosted the Chicago World's Fair of 1893, which was attended by nearly twenty-six million people and was considered to be the greatest exhibition of its kind in history. During this decade, the Christmas tree emerged as the star of the holiday season, aided by the invention of electricity. General Electric began to promote Christmas-tree lights to the American public. By 1900, Christmas had emerged as the most anticipated holiday in America.

LETTER HIGHLIGHTS
OF THE 1890S

TOY TERMINOLOGY

- *Roman candles*, requested by Wallace from Cloverport, Kentucky (page 65), are cylindrical fireworks that fire off a stream of brightly colored, shimmering stars.

- The *gum boots* requested by a child from Homestead, Vermont (page 70)—more popularly known as rain boots—are waterproof boots made of rubber that are typically worn in inclement weather.

- The *parlor croquet* set requested by Beulah of Brooklyn, New York (page 79), is a miniature version of the famous British pastime. Parlor games such as croquet, table tennis, and nine pins were popular domestic diversions for children around the turn of the twentieth century.

- The *milk wagon* desired by both Sophie of Brooklyn, New York (page 80), and Baby of Wales, United Kingdom (page 87), is a wheeled vehicle drawn by an animal that is used for delivering milk. The toy versions would have been drawn by a toy tin horse.

- The *wind-up train* desired by both Odie of Cloverport, Kentucky (page 68), and Marvin of Corsicana, Texas (page 88), might have been a model produced by E. R. Ives & Co., an American firm that became famous for its wind-up trains.

THE CHARM OF CHILDREN

As evidenced by two letters from this decade, children can be rather ambitious when it comes to Christmas wish lists. Hazel, of Lincoln, Nebraska (page 85), initially requests "two or three story books," but then, midsentence, corrects herself: "no, I'll say I want a hole library of books." Odie (page 68) realizes he isn't satisfied with the items he has just asked for (a story book, a little wagon, and the previously mentioned wind-up train). In fact, what he wants is "the whole earth."

LIVING HISTORY

- Young Milton of Fork Union, Virginia (page 83), writes, "As I am a believer in the Munro Doctrine please send me a good gun." Milton is referring to the foreign policy implemented by U.S. President James Monroe more than seventy years earlier, in the 1820s. The Monroe Doctrine states that any attempted European colonization of the American continents will be considered acts of political aggression by the United States government. Although a foundational principle of U.S. foreign policy in the nineteenth century, it nonetheless remains unclear what invading foreign powers young Milton is concerned about.

- Beulah (page 79) hopes that her visit to see Santa at Wechsler McNulty dry goods store in Brooklyn, New York, has improved her chances of him bringing her some gifts. The department store, which opened on September 16, 1893—a little more than a year before Beulah's visit—was located at the corner of Fulton Street and Bedford Avenue. It boasted oak finishes and elevators, and a full range of upscale merchandise, to the reported envy of the neighboring dry goods retailers.

WISH LIST TRENDS

Notice how the wish lists of the 1880s are filled with requests for fruits and nuts: Zilpah (page 66) wants "nuts, orange, raisins"; Marvin (page 88) asks for "oranges, apples and nuts"; Vivian (page 67) asks for "nuts and everything good"; and Fred (page 69) asks for "nuts" to be placed in his "stocking behind the coal stove."

DON'T MISS . . .

- *A girl's Christmas secret*. Her family, of New Orleans, Louisiana (page 74), has secretly put away money to buy Mama a pair of slippers, and the girl begs Santa Claus to keep this knowledge close to his heart, "cous all the money we got is to bye Ma a pare of slippers with don't let enybody see this letter becous the slipper business is secret."

- *Beula's kisses.* Beula of Lincoln, Nebraska (page 84), closes her letter with a postscript featuring two rows of Os, with three Os in each row. According to Beula, this enigmatic hieroglyphic represents affectionate kisses ("these are kisses").
- *Marvin's request for a rubber ball "that won't break window-glass."* Marvin (page 88) obviously learned the hard way about the window-breaking potential of rubber balls.

1891

Dear Good Santa Claus—

I have been so anxious to know how Santa Claus gets to so many houses in one night. I can't see how he accomplishes so much and have thought I would peep and see, but Mamy says it wid make him angry and he wont bring me anything next year. Mamy says one night as she lay in her trundle bed she thought she would peep, she has been sorry ever since, for he never came again, so please bring piano, pocket-book, seated wagon, books, roman candles, anything else you think will please me.

With love,

Wallace

1891

CHENAULT, KENTUCKY

Dear Santa Claus—

I am almost scared for fear my letter will be
to late for a chance for tho prize please send
me some candy, nuts, orange, raisins albam,
accordian bisque doll. I dont ask for anything
more I am a little school girl 10 years old.

Yours truly.

Zilpah

1891
CLOVERPORT, KENTUCKY

Dear Santa Claus—

I am not very large, but want a mighty heap of things. Leave the things in the dining-room for our Christmas tree, for if you were to bring the things down the chimney, I am afraid you will make a mistake and go to Grand-pa's room. Please bring me pocket-book, cart, bed, doll, book, candies, nuts and everything good, don't forget the baby.

Your loving

Vivian

1891

Dear Santa Claus—

I am a good boy and if you please sir, I want a big drum and a story book and I want a billy goat and a little wagon and a little wheel bar-row and I want a train what you wind up, that will run by itself and I want the whole earth.

Your little boy

Odie

1892

Dear Santa Claus:

My name is Fred. I live on Second street. I would like a pair of No. 9½ skates and a book about Samson, the strongest man in the world, and a coaster and some nuts and candies and I will hang my stocking behind the coal stove.

Fred

1892
HOMESTEAD, VERMONT

Dear Santa Cluss:

You are a kind man. I hoap you wont forget us. Homestead is a poor place. Dear Santa Cluss bring me some gum boots and then I don't want nothing more this year.

1892

Dear Santa Claus:

I thought I would write you a letter and tell you what my little brother and I want you to bring us for Christmas. My brother is four yaers old and I am seven years old. Johnnie is my brother's name and my name is May. Johnny wants you to bring him a baby doll, a tin horse, a drum and a little wagon. I want a ring, a doll baby, a new dress and a small hammock to put my baby doll in. We want you to come to our house on Christmas Eve. Our kindest regards to you, dear Santa Claus.

Your little friends,

Mary and Johnnie

1892

Dear Santa:

I would like you to bring me a large dolly and a doll buggy and a gold ring. Oh, dear Santa, please bring my brother Charlie, age 7 years, a new sled and please do not come down the dining room chimney because it is very hot. Please come down the parlor chimney.

Yours truly

Carrie

1892

DURHAM, NORTH CAROLINA

Dear Santa Claus—

I write to you so that you will know where I live. I live on Chapel Hill street! Please bring me a little stove and a doll bed. Good-bye.

Lillie

1893

My Dear Mr. Santa Claus,

crismas is pretty near and I want to try very hard and be a good girl so you will give me plenty of things. I want a white swis cap for Alberther. I want some game to play that won't require much geonies to play. I would also like a cloak for Alberther but that will fit all the childrens. Oh?!:" Mr. Santa Claus I'll be awfully good if you will only give me a tricycle for crismas. I won't ask anything else please, please" give me a tricycle or I will be so disap-pointed. I hope awfully you will bring me one. Please Mr. Santaclaus, grandma wants some cake and candy and I hain't got the money to grattify her wish cous all the money we got is to bye Ma a pare of slippers with don't let enybody see this letter becous the slipper business is secret. well I must stop good bye dear old Santaclaus good by.

P.S. don't forget My Tricicle for pity sakes don't forget.

1893

Dear "Santa Claus,"

I hope that the enclosed will be of some use to your fund. I am only twelve years old, so I cannot do very great things. The little dress I made out of a cast off jacket of my own, so "Santa Claus" must excuse me if there are rather more seams than there should be in a new one, but I think it will keep some poor little child warm. The toys I have had a long time, but I don't think they are much the worse for wear, as I have been very careful over them. Dear "Santa Claus," will you please tell me if I can come and see you distribute the things to the poor children?—But now I must close, wishing you every success in your scheme,

Blanche

1893

NEW HAVEN, CONNECTICUT

Dear Santa Claus:

As it is coming near Christmas I thought I would write you a short note, hoping to find you well and happy and that you will make me happy at Christmas by sending me a pair of skates and a jocky horse and a picture book and a watch and a open horse car.

With love,

Cornelius

1894
NEW YORK, NEW YORK

Dear Santa Claus:

Please be so kind and send six tickets of the Christmas-Tree Fund, for we are very poor, and my mamma can't buy us any clothes nor toys. I am fourteen years old and the oldest of six children. My father deserted us a year and a half ago, when my youngest brother was born. My poor mamma has to work very hard to keep us from starving, and so, dear Santa Claus, I hope you will not forget us and please don't forget my poor mamma.

Katie

P.S.—Rosie, Annie, Jakie, Herman and Johnny send their best regards.

1894

FORT WAYNE, INDIANA

Dear Santa Claus,

We herewith send you a dollar. Please buy some poor children something for Christmas.

Fene and Johnny

1894

Dear Santa Claus—

I do not expect any gifts for Christmas because my papa is out of work and mama says that Santa Claus does not come to poor people. But as I saw you up at Wechsler & McNulty's store I thought perhaps you would send me some. So anyhow I will tell you what I want, and hope you will send them: A pair of shoes No. 12C, a hat, a pair of mits, a pair of stockings, a pair of rubbers, a doll, a doll carriage, a game of parlor croquet, two boxes of candy, two gas balls, two sleighs, two books, three handkerchiefs. Now, dear Santa Claus, I do hope you will send this and anything else you want to, for I'm afraid if I ask for too many I won't get any. I'm 7 years old and I believe in Santa Claus, though so many children don't. Now goodby, dear Santa.

Yours lovingly,

Beulah

P.S.—If you will send some presents to my sisters, Ina, Mona and Hellen, and my brother Irving, who is a baby, I would be very glad.

1894

BROOKLYN, NEW YORK

Dear Old Santa Claus—

You have so many nice presents it is hard to select one, so wont you do it for a very nice little girl and send it to Monroe street on Christmas eve? It would be appreciated and taken good care of, especially if it was a milk wagon.

Yours truly,

Sophie

1894

BROOKLYN, NEW YORK

Dear Santa Claus—

I write to you a few lines, hoping you are well, as I suppose you are, as I hope you are, and I want you to come to my house Christmas eve, which is on Pacific street, and will you bring me what I want, which is as follows: A drum, a box of building blocks, and a pair of kid gloves. Dear Santa, my name is Johnnie and I am 6 years old, and am a very good boy and will always be if I live. I close my letter by saying goodby, and hope you will bring me what I want. Goodby.

To Santa from

Johnnie

1895

STEELTON, PENNSYLVANIA

Dear Santa Claus:

You dear old fellow won't you please bring me a
ring, an Epworth League pin, red jacket, mink,
gloves, muff, and that ain't enough. Good-bye
old Santa, I love you so.

Jean

1895

FORK UNION, VIRGINIA

Mister Santa Claus:

As I am a believer in the Munro Doctrine please send me a good gun.

Milton

1895

RICHMOND, VIRGINIA

Dear Santa Claus:

When you come to Richmond, please stop your reindeer on the top of West Main St and when you show yourself down our chimney have in your pack something for

John

1896

LINCOLN, NEBRASKA

Dear santa Caus:

I want a big doll and a doll carriage and a tablet.

Beula
000
000
these are kisses

1896
LINCOLN, NEBRASKA

Dear Santa Claus:

I live on Q street and I guess I will write you a letter. I want a sled, a doll, all kinds of games, and two or three story books, no, I'll say I want a hole library of books. I want some paper dolls and all the furniture that I need to furnish my house with. I want a bycl and a pair of skatts and I want snow and cold weather. I guess I have finished my letter now so goodbye. I must close Dear Santa Claus.

From a little girl that wishes to be your friend.

Hazel

1897

SCOTLAND, UNITED KINGDOM

Dear Santa Claus,

I want a doll and a coach. That is all.

1898

Dear Santa Claus,

I want a hores with a big tail and a big mane, and eyes and nose and mouth, and a bridle and saddl. A.B.C. book and a crain, and a horn and a cowboy doll, a little waggon and a tule box and some nials and a milk wagon and some candy, apples, oranges, bananas.

From your friend Baby

1899

CORSICANA, TEXAS

Dear Santa Claus:

I am 7 years old. I want a hammer, nails, race-horse and train that you wind up, rubber ball that won't break window-glass, a little drum, hobby horse, a bunch of firecrackers, oranges, apples, candy and nuts.

Your friend,

Marvin

1899

HOWE, TEXAS

Dear Santa Claus:

I want a big doll, a pair of vases, a doll buggy and a doll bed, some candy, nuts, a set of dishes, a silver spoon, knife and fork. So good-bye. Aged 10.

Myra

1899

DENVER, COLORADO

Dear Santa Claus—

I write to let you know that I was very thankful for what you give me last Christmas. And the nice wagon that you brought me got stolen from me and This Christmas I would like to have a tool chest so that I may make a wagon and a sledge so I can carry mama clouths on them An a pair of shoes please. I am a poor boy and I would like to help my mother much as I can and she has to wash and iron for a liven. And she is not strong. I will close. Good bye.

I live on Twenty-first street and my name is William

1899

GARLAND, TEXAS

Dear old sweet Santa Claus:

I want you to bring me a gun, a little black dog,
and bring Sister Nannie a black cat and doll.

With best wishes.

Bobbie

1899

Dear Santa—

I tought I wood wite a few lines I want a stable
and some oranges and some candy I want a
cane and a par gloves.

Tom

LETTERS

1900

1909

The 1900s were a decade of revolutionary innovation in Europe and America. Einstein launched modern physics when he introduced his theory of special relativity, Freud theorized the laws of the unconscious in *The Interpretation of Dreams*, and Picasso inaugurated the modern art era with his painting *Les Demoiselles d'Avignon*. America became a hotbed of technological invention. In 1903, Wilbur and Orville Wright made the first manned plane flight in history; and in 1908, the first Model T was built at the Ford plant in Detroit, ushering in the automobile era. Frank Baum's recently published *The Wizard of Oz* was read aloud by many Christmas firesides, along with O. Henry's touching short story "The Gift of the Magi." In the realm of domestic politics, President Theodore Roosevelt's son Archie stole the holiday spotlight. In 1902, with no Christmas tree having been ordered for the White House, little Archie installed one in a closet with the help of a carpenter. He strung it with gifts for his family, who were much surprised by Archie's ingenuity when he shared it with them on Christmas morning. The charm of children, indeed!

LETTER HIGHLIGHTS
OF THE 1900S

TOY TERMINOLOGY

- The *Punch & Judy* desired by Gordon of Manitoba, Canada (page 110), refers to a miniature theater and a cast of puppets—among them, Mr. Punch and his wife, Judy. With this toy, Gordon would have performed the Punch and Judy Show for family and friends, a puppet theater tradition that dates back to seventeenth-century England.

- A girl from Reno, Nevada (page 105), requests "silver hartes to put on my chain bracelet." This *chain bracelet*, also known as a charm bracelet, would have been a piece of jewelry adorned with "fobs" or symbolic pendants. Tiffany & Co.'s iconic charm bracelet, introduced in 1889—eleven years before this child made her request to Santa—helped spur the popularity of this jewelry in America.

- The *hobby horse* requested by Kyle of Flagstaff, Arizona (page 117), is a toy that dates back to medieval times. It consisted of a wooden stick with a replica of a horse's head appended to one end. Children would straddle the stick and gallop around, "riding" the hobby horse.

- The boy from Aberdeen, South Dakota (page 121), who requested a *loop-the-loop* is likely referring to a miniature replica of the famous Coney Island roller coaster "Loop the Loop," which operated from 1901 to 1910. Amusement parks were a significant part of American popular culture at the turn of the twentieth century, and many toys of the time were modeled after well-known rides.
- Allen of Manitoba, Canada (page 113), requests two types of pencils: *lad* (or lead) and *slate pencils*. Slate pencils, cut from soft slate or soapstone, were introduced in the middle of the nineteenth century and employed by schoolchildren to write on slate tablets up until the early twentieth century. Lead pencils—which were actually made from graphite, not lead—became wildly popular after the Civil War and were used by schoolchildren, businesses, and artists alike.
- The *skate key* requested by William of Washington, District of Columbia (page 124), was a small key used to tighten the fit of ice skates or roller skates.
- *Little Women*, requested by Juanita of Ardmore, Oklahoma (page 118), was one of the most popular American fiction books of the late nineteenth century. Written by Louisa May Alcott and first

published in two volumes in 1868 and 1869, it narrates the journey of four sisters from youth to womanhood.

- The *tocking doll* (or talking doll) that sisters Pattie and Sarah of Manitoba, Canada (page 104), requested had just hit the market at the turn of the twentieth century. The first talking doll was introduced by the Jumeau Company of France in 1894. Using phonograph technology, it had a working vocabulary of thirty-five words, and could sing and tell stories.

THE CHARM OF CHILDREN

The letter writers of this decade are particularly careful to flaunt their finest manners while appealing to Santa's generosity. Allen (page 113) politely inquires, "How do you like it in the snow?" Marjorie (page 101), having requested "a little bureau with a glass on it," offers Santa her thanks in advance: "I thank you, my kind friend." William (page 124) closes his letter with distinguished formality: "I remain yours truly." Pattie and Sarah (page 104) assure Santa of their devotion: "We love you best of all." But most impressive is Muriel (page 107), whose efforts are sure to be rewarded by Santa with a surplus of toys. She writes, "How have you been?

I hope you have been very well so it would not put you back in your work? And how is dear Mrs. Criss Cringel I hope she is well she is such a dear old lady. Dear Santa Claus I do not want to ask you for very many things. Because I do not want to impose on such good nachur."

Other letter writers adopt a different strategy. Rather than advertise his exemplary behavior in order to convince Santa to bring him more gifts, Donald (page 108) begins his letter by admitting to a mixed character: "Sometimes I'm good and sometimes I'm naughty." Despite his lapses, he humbly strives to advance the good: ". . . but if you will excuse me I'll try to be much better."

LIVING HISTORY

- The *teddy bear* requested by Edith of Portland, Oregon (page 120), and L. Q. of Los Angeles, California (page 125), was named after President Theodore Roosevelt. The president, on a hunting trip with friends in 1902—a few years before these letters were written—was said to have famously spared the life of a bear. Inspired by Teddy's generosity, Brooklyn merchant Morris Michtom produced the nation's first stuffed "Teddy bear." By the time Edith and L. Q. wrote their letters (in 1907 and 1908 respectively), the teddy bear had become one of the most popular gifts of the era.

- The earthquake that Edna of San Francisco, California (page 119), alludes to—she writes, "We have had no tree since the earthquake and we lived in a shack until a few days ago"—was one of the worst natural disasters in U.S. history. Occurring on Wednesday, April 18, 1906 (a year and a half before Edna wrote her letter), the earthquake and the ensuing fire destroyed more than 80 percent of San Francisco and is believed to have caused more than three thousand deaths.

DON'T MISS . . .

- *Thelma's request for a small army of cats*. She would prefer more, but at her mother's advice, she only requests six—a half dozen being thought sufficient to do battle with the pesky mice that share her family home in Owensboro, Kentucky (page 116). She asks for "a half dozen cats now Dear Santa I will not ask for more Mama says six cats will be a plenty although there are good many mice at our home . . ."
- *Gracie's charming lack of curiosity about the visitor from the North Pole*. Rather than stay up all night to catch a glimpse of Santa putting presents

under the tree—the sleep-depriving desire of most children—Gracie of Jonesboro, Arkansas (page 126), prefers to get a good night's rest. "Santa," she writes, "I would rather have you come while I am asleep."

1900

CENTERVILLE, MONTANA

Santa:

I asked you last Christmas to bring me a doll bureau with a looking glass on it. I guess you didn't get the letter. Mamma told me that sometimes the letters can't get up to your house in the ice. Mamma told me to-day that you could get the letter now, so I ask you to bring me a little bureau with a glass on it. Mamma said that I need not ask for more, so I thank you my kind friend.

Truly your little girl.

Marjorie

1900

Dnar Santa Claun,

I will tell you what I want for Christmas Please bring me a doll and a doll bed and a ring and a thimble Mamama says that I want a good many of present. I am to sick to go to school. I have not been to school since last Thursday. I am seven years old. good by.

Ruby

1900
CLEVELAND, OHIO

Dear Santa Claus:

I am a poor little girl. And haven't much money to spend, so I hope you will remember me on your travels, as I will remember you in my prayers. Liberty St. Up stairs.

1900

WALKERVILLE, MONTANA

Dear St. Nick—

You may bring me a toy piano, a doll cradle, a box of chocolates and a pair of 10-cent mittens. My mamma will get me a dress and a doll. My brother told me she would.

1900

MANITOBA, CANADA

Dear Santa—

Will you please bring me and Sarah a tocking doll and a small musicing box. We love you best of all.

Pattie and Sarah

1900

RENO, NEVADA

Dear Santa Claus

For Christmas I want a little doll like Ethel and a big enough cradle for my other dolls and some hand ker chiefs and a work basket and some silver hartes to put on my chain bracelet.

1901
MINNEAPOLIS, MINNESOTA

Dear Santie Claus:

Pleas send me a new dress and a par of shoes and mybrother some shoes for he has not got any I am 10 years old and my brother is 5 yearse and Dear Santa pleas send a par of mittens for both of uss for our hands is awful cold and don't forget the little boyes and girls that is poor like we are.

1901
HONOLULU, HAWAII

Dear Santa Claus:

How have you been? I hope you have been very well so it would not put you back in your work? And how is dear Mrs. Criss Cringel I hope she is well she is such a dear old lady. Dear Santa Claus I do not want to ask you for very many things. Because I do not want to impose on such good nachur.

And would you please give me a doll's bed and a doll's burea. And would you please fill all the other little girls' and boy's stockings and if you have not enough for a poor girl or boy's stocking please take some out of mine so you can fill theirs full.

With lots of love from your little friend

Muriel

1901
HONOLULU, HAWAII

My Dear Santa Claus:

Sometimes I'm good and some times I'm naughty, but if you will excuse me I'll try to be much better. Please send me a box of Turtles and Ducks and other little things inside the box too. And I would like a little writing desk as I'm learning to write.

Donald

1902

NEW SOUTH WALES, AUSTRALIA

Dear Santa Claus,

Christmas week will soon be here now, and I would like to ask you to bring me a nice toy. I would like a gun best, so if you have one in your bundles of pretty things, you leave it for the baby at our house; if you haven't got a gun, bring me something else nice.

1902

NEW SOUTH WALES, AUSTRALIA

Dear Santa Claus,

Christmas is coming, the ducks are getting fat. Please put a penny in the little boy's hat. If you haven't a peney, a hapenny will do; if you haven't a hapenny, a farthing will do; and we will bless you. Mother wants something good; I want a motor car, and that's all.

1903

MANITOBA, CANADA

Dear Santa Claus,

Will you send me a drum, a bugle, Punch and Judy, a gun, magic lantern, candys, apples, oranges and nuts.

Yours,

Gordon

1903
RICHMOND, VIRGINIA

Dear Sandy Claus:

Please bring me a dog on rollers and a nice little horse on rollers and some candy, nuts and rasons and some fireworks. Dear old sandy, I have so many things I don't want much. I will try and be a good boy. Now, please hurry up and come and don't forget me, so good by from your sweet little boy.

Albert

1903

My Dear Santa—

I would like lots of things, but most of all I would like a large doll which will open and shut its eyes and will cry when you squeeze it. I would also like a pair of skates, and lots of candy, nuts and oranges.

Now, Santa, our chimney is very small. I wanted my papa to have it made larger, but he would not do it. So I will leave the window of the west room open so you can come in there. You will see my stocking hanging up by the window. Now, hoping you will please not to forget me. I am your little friend.

V. F.

1903

MANITOBA, CANADA

Dear Santa Claus,

Allen wants a watch, and a bugle, and a little horse and wagon, and a little gun and caps, and a ball, and he doo not want any more drums. But he want a picture book, and a mouth-organ, and a pencil box, and a cup and saucea, and set of blocks, and a box of lad pencils, and a box of slate pencils, and a song book. How do you like it in the snow?

Allen

1904
ALTOONA, PENNSYLVANIA

Dear Santa Claus, Altoona Pa:

I thought i would write you a few lines to let you no what i want for Christmas. i want a ice wagon with to horses in and a express wagon and a drum and a horn and lots of candy and nuts.

Larence

1904

Dear Santa Claus—

Please bring me a nice doll with black hair, and some candy and nuts and raisins and an orange and a pair of slippers for me and David and my dolly and a nice pair for papa, size eight. And a new pair of shoes for mamma and a pair of kid gloves for Isabel, and some peppermints for the grandpas and grandmas, and that's all I can think of, but if you think of anything nice for good little girls bring them too.

Wilma

P.S.—I forgot to tell you to bring a new wrist bag for mamma. Good-bye. And a new bag for papa's money.

1905

OWENSBORO, KENTUCKY

Dear Santa

I want a little piano so I can sing and play for Papa and Mamma a rocking horse a little Iron so I can iron my dollies clothes and a half dozen cats now Dear Santa I will not ask for any more Mama says six cats will be a plenty although there are good many mice at our home so I will not write any more hoping you will not forget my name and number

Thelma

1906

FLAGSTAFF, ARIZONA

Dear Old Santa Claus:

I want a sled and some candy and nuts, I want a bank to put all my money in that I earn myself and I want a gun for Christmas. For my brother he wants an automobile, a wagon that you hawl barrels in, a hobby horse, an engine and a box of tools for Christmas. Good bye Santa Claus.

Your friend,

Kyle

1907

ARDMORE, OKLAHOMA

Dear Santa:

I want to thank you for nice things that you have always brought me, and want to ask you for some more favors. Please bring me a signet ring, and a book called Little Wmen. I hope you will remember the little children.

Juanita

1907

SAN FRANCISCO, CALIFORNIA

Dear Santa Claus—

I thought I would write to you to let you know
I have moved, and I hope you won't forget me
this year. I would like a doll's buggy and my
stocking full and a Christmas tree. We have
had no tree since the earthquake and we lived
in a shack until a few days ago. I also have a
little sister 6 years old and a little brother,
and he is 8 years old. She would like the same.
Her name is Genevive and my brother's name
is Willie. He would like a drum and a bicycle
and both his stockings filled. Willie has been
sick but he feels better now. Papa would have
sent you some money but he has been out of
work lately. Dear Santa Claus, please do not
forget us this year. I hope you will fit down our
chimney as we have no mantel this year.

Edna

1907

PORTLAND, OREGON

Dear Santa Clause:

I thought I would write and tell you what I want for Christmas. I want a big teddy bear. I am only 7 years old. that is al I want for Christmus.

Your frend

Edith

1907

Dear Santa Claus:

Are you coming to see me this Christmas? You came to see me last year and I thank you for all the nice things you brought me. I have been quite a good boy. This year I would like a pair of overshoes, a loop-the-loop, a little train, some candy and nuts. I am so tickled I can't think of anything else, but I will like anything else you bring me.

P.S. We have a fireplace and my stockings will be small.

P.S. I want a box of bon bons like sister's.

1908
PENSACOLA, FLORIDA

Dear Kris Kringle—

I am a little boy six years old. Would you please bring me a wheel-barrow, whistle, marble, hammer and everything from a monkey on a string to a bright tin hopping toad.

Your loving friend,

Stephen

1908
ANAHEIM, CALIFORNIA

Dear Santa Claus—

I was reading in *The Herald* what good you are doing for the poor children. I have no shoes and no father and I am 9 years old. I have a little brother 4 years. My mother works hard for our living and she doesn't get much for her washing, and I expect nothing for Christmas. I wish you would send me a pair of No. 2 shoes. My mother wishes a pair of No. 3½.

Miss J. L.

1908

Dear Santa:

Please bring me a pair of ball berring skates, a horn, drum, catchers glove, box of dominoes box of checkers, low sleigh, tool chest, fill my stockings with good things. I promise in return for these things, to be a good boy and to mind my mother and father. I would like to have a 10 cent skate key

Thanking you I remain yours truly

little William

1908

LOS ANGELES, CALIFORNIA

Dear Santa—

My sister wrote you and I am afraid you may forget me, like last year when you did not come. I want a Teddy bear and a coat and warm dress. My sister needs a coat. It is cold when we go to school. My little brother is 3 years and has no clothes or shoes. He wants a little wagon. Please, dear Santa, don't forget to come this year. I am 6 years; my sister is 8 and my brother is 3. The door will be open.

L. Q.

1908

Dear Santy—

I am a little girl 8 years old and I want a doll and a doll buggy and some candy and nuts, Santa I would rather have you come while I am asleep, I live on the corner of Front and Alice street.

Don't forget me my name is Gracie.

1908

PENSACOLA, FLORIDA

Dear Santa—

I want something that you can wind up and will run. Please bring it to me, and I want an orange, apple and some candy. I want something I can have fun with. I don't know just what, but what you think I ought to have.

J. K.

1909

Dear santa

I ana little 9 year old Boy i wood lik to Haf a
par of shoes a new wast and a par of Pance and
a sled if corse i like candy and son nuts please
dont for git ny Brother He is 12 years old i liv
Wells St.

Walter

good By santa.

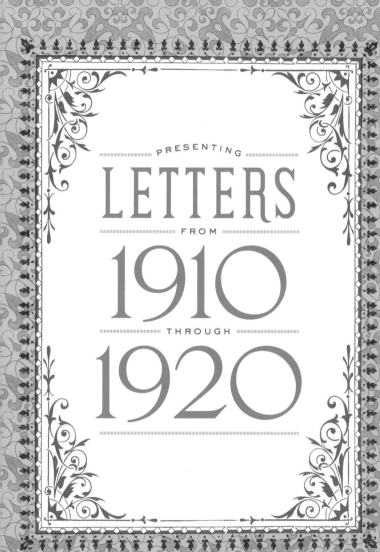

PRESENTING

LETTERS

FROM

1910

THROUGH

1920

1910–1920

The 1910s were dominated by the fighting of the First World War, a global conflict that forever altered the political structure of Europe. The assassination of Archduke Franz Ferdinand on June 28, 1914 led to the outbreak of the Great War on July 28, 1914. The first troops from the United States arrived in Europe in the summer of 1917 and remained until Armistice Day on November 11, 1918, when the Allies signed a ceasefire agreement with Germany. Woodrow Wilson became the first U.S. president to travel to Europe while still in office when he attended the Paris Peace Conference in Versailles, which began in January 1919. Despite the war, Christmas spirits during this decade were high, even penetrating the battlefield itself. In 1914, British and German soldiers agreed to cease hostilities for the duration of the holiday, a spontaneous peace known as the Christmas Truce—proof that holiday peace and goodwill can illuminate even the darkest hours of history.

LETTER HIGHLIGHTS
FROM 1910 THROUGH 1920

TOY TERMINOLOGY

- The *baby bump*, requested by Ida of Chanute, Kansas (page 145), was a baby doll from doll-maker E. I. Horsman's "Can't Break Em" line. Baby Bumps dolls, which the company introduced in 1910 and marketed as being resistant to bumps and breakage, featured a lifelike painted head and a cloth body stuffed with cork.

- Isobel of Ontario, Canada (page 164), requests a *game of lotto*, referring to the board game Lotto. A game of chance with rules similar to bingo, Lotto was produced by the Milton Bradley Company, maker of American classics such as Chutes & Ladders and Candyland.

- The *tamoshanter* (or Tam o' Shanter) requested for their dolls by sisters Margaret and Catherine of Rockford, Illinois (page 169), refers to a plaid wool cap with a pom-pom affixed to the top. It was known by this name in nineteenth-century Scotland, where it was inspired by the hero of the Robert Burns poem "Tam o' Shanter," published in 1791.

- The *tinker toys* requested by Charles of Hillmont, Wyoming (page 173), refer to a construction set that came with parts such as wheels, caps, pulleys, and sticks that could be assembled in various ways, enabling children to create imaginative designs. Tinker Toys were first issued in 1914 and are still in production today.

- Both Andrey of Anderson, South Carolina (page 156), and Sheila of Victoria, Australia (page 161), request a *celluloid doll*, which would have been made of an inexpensive, easily moldable, early form of plastic. Developed in the late 1800s, celluloid was originally used as a replacement for ivory and soon was featured in a range of products, from cheap jewelry to buttons to kitchen items.

WISH LIST TRENDS

Notice the multiple appearances of the automobile on Christmas wish lists in this decade. James (page 137), Annie (page 138), and Earle (page 150) each requested one. Henry Ford introduced the affordable, mass-produced Model T in 1908, and cars quickly became a central feature of American culture in the 1910s.

LIVING HISTORY

- As the letters of this decade attest, World War I, which lasted from 1914 to 1918, entered into the consciousness of the children of the era and provoked a mature, gracious humanity in many young hearts. Sheila in Australia (page 161) worries that the war may have taken its toll on Santa himself and offers to forsake her own presents for his sake: "I hope this dreadful war has not made you any poorer, for, if it has, I would willingly do without any presents for myself." She asks Santa to give special consideration to the children affected by the war: "give an extra gift or two to the poor little Belgian and Servian boys and girls who have suffered so much; and also to some of our brave Australia boys in the trenches." She closes her letter with a tender gesture of generosity: "if you do not bring me quite so many presents this year, or even none at all, I shall try not to be disappointed, for I shall say, 'Santa Claus is giving them to the little boys and girls in Europe, who have been made so miserable and unhappy by this awful war.'"

- Howard (page 154), writing in 1914 at the beginning of the war, is aware that difficult times lie ahead: "Since the war is on and times are so hard I wlil only ask for a fiew Things." Nancy (page 166), writing in 1918, celebrates the war's end with a touching tribute: "I hope all the little Girls and

Boys in France and Belgium will have a happy Xmas now the War is done."

DON'T MISS . . .

- *Donald's sociability.* Donald (page 147), perhaps unaware of Santa's busy holiday schedule, invites him to a local church event, the can't-miss party of the Petrolia, Kansas, Christmas season: "We are going to have a Christmas tree at the church next Tuesday night and you want to be there."

- *Ethel's realism.* Ethel of Springfield, Illinois (page 152), rather than requesting any specific gifts for herself, defers the decision to Santa Claus on account of her idiosyncratic habits of attendance: "I have not went to Sunday school as regular as I have ought to, so I think I ought not to be choicy about my present."

- *Eston's steadfast faith in the existence of Santa Claus.* Despite the aggressive skepticism of his peers—"the boys in school try to fool me and try to make me believe you are a joke"—Eston of Laurens, South Carolina (page 136), remains unshaken in his Christmas convictions: "I still believe in you."

- *Orion's stealthy stratagem.* Orion of Laurens, South Carolina (page 139), asks Santa to skip the publicity of a visit to the family's living room and instead just leave "two pecks of big oranges" under the "front door-steps," a spot where only Orion can find them: "so I can slip under there, and eat to my heart aches." And he promises to play it cool after his secret feast: "Then I'll go back to playing as if I had done nothing."

1910

LAURENS, SOUTH CAROLINA

Dear Old Santa Claus:

You have never failed to come and I know you will come again but the boys in school try to fool me and try to make me believe you are a joke and it is only the Old Folks at home I still believe in you.

With love,

Eston

1910

Dear Santie Claus:

This is my first letter to you. I am a little boy 5 years olde and are oflie sweet two, that is what my aunt Ella tells me every day Now I will tell you what I would like very much to have, a little train, horne, Irish mail, fire works, candies, oranges, nuts. Now don't forget my two little brothers Harry and Robert, I think Robert wants a rubber doll and bring Harry the same, and dont forget to bring mama and papa a automobeal and aunt something nice to.

So good by,

James

1910

SYRACUSE, NEW YORK

Dear Santa Claus—

I am a little girl 6 years old and I am in the first grade at school but the snow is so deep I can not go now as we have a mile to walk so be sure and call at my house and bring me a new pair of rubbers for Xmas, a wagon, automobile a doll's stove, a doll's high chair, a doll's rocking cair and some hair ribbons also bring me some candy nuts and oranges. I guess you think I wants a lot of things But please dont for get my school teacher her name is Miss Labring We all like her very much so dont forget her.

From a little friend.

Annie

1910
LAURENS, SOUTH CAROLINA

Dear Santa Claus:

Will you come and travel down our clean chimney and leave under our front door-steps just about two pecks of big oranges so I can slip under there, and eat to my heart aches. Then I'll go back playing as if I had done nothing.

Orion

1910

Dear Santa Claus:

Please bring me a "Jim" suit and a doll and some "scates". Please bring me a set of dolls dishes and a doll carriage and a fairy tale book and a lot of other books and a gold neck chain and a gold bracelet for Christmas.

From your loving friend.

1911

LAVERGNE, TENNESSEE

My Dearest Santa:

I am a little boy and I want you to know I am not dead but am still alive and go to school every day. I am in the 4-B grade. My teacher says I am a good little boy, so you should remember me. I want you to bring me a hat, pair of kid gloves, all kinds of fruits and fireworks: don't forget my teacher and his children, and my ex-teacher, Miss Inthia, of Murfreesboro, and my schoolmates and nieces, W. B. and R. C. They live on Second avenue. Don't forget my mother, father, brother, sister and grandpa.

Your one little boy.

M. L.

1911

Dear Santa:

I would like you to bring me a doll about two feet high. I would also like a doll bed for the doll. Please bring me the book called "The Mill on the Floss." Don't forget me in candy, fruits and fireworks. Papa says that I am a naughty little girl, but I try to be good, so please don't judge me by outward appearance.

Your little friend,

Burnice

1911

NASHVILLE, TENNESSEE

Dear Santa Claus:

I am a little boy as fat as can be. So bring me a pair of roller skates and plenty to eat. And please remember my friends, Ardelle and Irene, Misses Eugene and Mattie and brothers, Lawrence and Lee.

Your little boy,

Walter

1911

MONTGOMERY, ALABAMA

Dear Santa:

Please bring me a bicycle and lots of other things if you think that I have been good enough. If I have been extra good, as I have tried to me, please bring me some fireworks, too. I will try to be good next year, so that you won't forget me.

Your little friend,

Willie

1912

CHANUTE, KANSAS

Dear Santa Claus.

I want a doll and doll bugy I am a little girl seven years old. I want acndy, nuts and oranges. Oh yes I want a baby bump.

Your loving friend

Ida

FROM A PAIR OF SISTERS

Dear Santy Claus,

I am a little girl six years old and I am good too And I would like for you to bring me a cloack and a pair of shoes I am bare footed and some toys and frute. goodby hoping you will bring them.

Annie L.

P.S. Irene is my sister.

Dear Santy

I am sick in bed and would be so glad to have something my ma is a widow and I want you to bring me a cloak and some toys and frute. goodby hoping you will bring them

a little girl

Irene L.

1912

PETROLIA, KANSAS

Dear Santa Claus.

I am going to write you a letter telling what I want for Christmas. I want a pair of gloves, a bicycle and a light for my bicycle. Papa has not said what he wanted nor neither has mamma. But you bring what you thin kbest. My little sister wants a set of furs. We are going to have a Christmas tree at the church next Tuesday night and you want to be there and give me my present as well as mamma's, and papa's and sister's.

Your little friend

Donald

1912

Dear Santa Claus—

This Christmas I would like you to bring me a toboggan, and a pair of red gloves, a story book, and about two yards of hair ribbon. I would like the ribbon to be dark red and the toboggan to be red and white.

Santa, you know that I have not missed a Sunday school and I always try to be a good girl all the time.

Don't forget to bring me some nuts and candy and some oranges.

And Santa, don't forget other children. So good-bye Santa, because I know you got to go to many other places.

Your 12 year old friend,

Mollie

1912

CORNING, IOWA

Dear Santa Claus:

Dear Santa the weather is colder now Christmas will be here soon. I wish I had a twenty two so I could go a hunting Christmas. And I wish the water would freeze long before Christmas so I could go skating. I want a pair of new skates this Christmas. My old ones are getting too old for me. The days are getting shorter very fast now. I have named about all the presents I want now.

Good by your friend

George

1912

CHANUTE, KANSAS

Dear Old Santa:

I am a little boy six years old. I wan you to visit my house on Christmas Eve. I want a horse, a ball, a drum, a horn, a book, an automobile and a train of cars. Bring my sisters something nice and my little dog a bone.

Your friend

Earle

1912

Dear Santa Claus—

We live out at Big Cottonwood canyon by the power house. Papa has not worked for a long time; he has gone somewhere to look for work. Please come and see us. We are four kiddos. Lettie Mae is 15 years and wants a doll. Louise is 10 years and wants a doll and box of ribbons and candy and story book. Vando is 8 years and wants a sled and some candy. Baby, 2 years, wants rag doll and candy. And oblige

Lettie Mae

Please come.

1912
SPRINGFIELD, ILLINOIS

Dear Santa Claus—

My name is Ethel. I am 14 years old. I live on East Cook street. I have not went to Sunday school as regular as I have ought to, so I think I ought not to be choicy about my present.

Yours truly,

Ethel

1913
SAN FRANCISCO, CALIFORNIA

Dear Santa Claus,

bring me three drumsticks—two for my drum and one for my mouth.

Little Tommy

1913

LEWISTON, MAINE

Dear Santa Claus:

My papa is having a hard time, he is picking up wood to get along with. I thank you for the stuff you brought us last Christmas. This Christmas I want a pair of roller skates and a game and a book of Jack the Giant Killer and a boy's sled. Remember I have a brother about 7 years old. He wants a car that winds up and Jack the Giant Killer and a box of candy and a boy's sled. this is for my little brother. Good-bye for this time.

This is a little boy eight years old that is writing this. My brother is younger. My name is

Charles

1914

Dear Santa Claus:

Since the war is on and times are so hard I wlil only ask for a fiew Things I want a foot-ball a gun and a Set of Carpenters tools and candy and fruit Wishing you a merry-Xmas

Your little friend

Howard

1914

IDAHO FALLS, IDAHO

Dear Santa Claus:

When you are on your journey through this country stop at my home and give me a doll and doll buggy, an automobile, a small water gun, and oblige your little girl.

Edna

P.S.—I also want a train.

1914

Dear Santa Claus:

My little sister wants a celouid dooll and I want a dool and carrige and bed and my little sister want a cow that will holer and I want a lot of fruit from your friends

Andrey

1914

NEWPORT, RHODE ISLAND

Dear Santa Claus

Would you please give me a scarf and cup for
Christmas I will be much obliged if you do
my age is 10 years. My father is dead and my
mother is working. I will Cose your's

1915

Dear Santa Claus,

I am a good little boy and I would love for you to bring me a knife and a wagon and a little train and some candy and some little fire crackers. I have a sweet little brother three years old he wants you to bring him a little wagon and a little horse and some fruit please Santa Claus dont forget us we will go to bed early and shut our eyes tight we wont look and we will be good from little

Lloyd and Bunny

1915
ELYRIA, OHIO

Dear Father Christmas

This is my first Christmas in America I would like you to send me a sled

Reggie

1915
TACOMA, WASHINGTON

Dear Santa Claus:

Will you please bring me something for Christmas. I am a boy 8 years old and I wish you would bring my brother something to he is 6 years old and his name is Arnold my pap been sick to I have a baby sister just 12 days old I wish you would bring her something to from your little friend

Jimie

1916
QUEBEC, CANADA

Hello Dear Santie—

Well, dear Santie, you want to make your reindeers fly if you want to get through with all those children who have written you but I hope you won't forget to call on myself and two little sisters. Their names are Isabell and Annie May, also little Brother George. Now, Dear Santie, I am not going to tell you what to bring us as you know what little boys and girls like best. Hope you will take time to read this letter.

From your friend,

Jean

1916

Dear Santa Claus,

I hope you are still alive, as it is getting very near the time when you should come to my bedside with a few of your nice Xmas presents. I hope this dreadful war has not made you any poorer, for, if it has, I would willingly do without any presents for myself if you could manage to give an extra gift or two to the poor little Belgian and Servian boys and girls who have suffered so much; and also to some of our brave Australia boys in the trenches. Please don't send them my dolls, for I don't think they would care for them. Chocolates and cigarettes are more in their line. Before closing I must thank you for last year. Perhaps as you have so many little boys and girls to attend to, you may have forgotten; so I will tell you. They are one nice large doll, one doll's bath together with a little celluloid doll to float on the water in and one tennis racket. But if you do not bring me quite so many presents this year, or even none at all,

I shall try not to be disappointed, for I shall say, "Santa Claus is giving them to the little boys and girls in Europe, who have been made so miserable and unhappy by this awful war." Hoping you will live as long as there are any little boys and girls in the world.

I remain, your sincere and expectant friend.

Sheila

P.S. Please notice that my address is the same as last year.

1916

Dear Santa Claus:

I will write you a little letter and see if you will remember me at Christmas, as we are poor and have no father. I also have a crippled little brother who has only one leg. My mother goes out working every day to make a living. I would like very much for you to send me a pair of nice warm mittens and also some stockings and a few toys. Do not forget my good mother and my crippled brother.

1916

Santa Dear:

I would like very much for Christmas if you have enough things for me, I would like a game of table croquet for Christmas and some other games. I would like some nice books to. I do not want a doll or a carrige because I think I am getting to big for them and you might give them to some poor little girl or boy. Because they may not have any doll or anything and I have a doll and carrige. I think I have every thing I want. I have a desk, a doll, acarrage and a game of lotto.

So I think I have enough.

You need not come to me if you have not enough because I would sooner you give them to some poor little girls and boys that have not anything.

I hope you have a happy Christmas.

I remain yours,

Isobel

P. S. Aged 10 years. A Happy Christmas Santie.

1917
EL PASO, TEXAS

Mr. Santa Claus, Ice Land.

Please brig me a dolly. And please, Mr. Santa, brig it up the steem heeter, and not down the chimney, so she won't get her hair burned.

1917
EL PASO, TEXAS

Last Year I wrote a nice letter, and you never answered it. I told you to bring me a little baby sister. So please send her to me this year. Also a pair of real diamond earrings for my mamma.

1918

Dear Santa Claus,

It is nearly Xmas time, So I must write to you, our else you might for-get to call on Xmas Eve. I think Xmas is just the loveliest time. We always have such fun and lots of things for dinner and tea. Some times we go down to see Grandma. We love the trip in the car and train. You never forget to come and bring us just the things we ask you for. I know you never for-got the little children over at the War. We always send you money to help to buy toys and clothes for them. I bet they like Xmas time too. And you never for-get the soldiers. I hope you will bring me another book and a Knitting bag. I have read all my books. We spent a nice Xmas last year and after it was over we went to Ballarat for a holiday. I was sorry when it was time to come home. I hope all the little Girls and Boys in France and Belgium will have a happy Xmas now the War is done. I am sending you a shilling for the cot fund to buy some toys. I will say good by now because Jess and Margery are going to write to you. I hope you will have a jolly Xmas.

With lots of love from

Nancy
Age 6 years 10 months.

Don't forget to bring father and Mother something nice.

1919
MOUNTAINAIR, NEW MEXICO

Dear Santa Claus:

Please bring me a Red Cross car. or a wagon.

Dear Santa Claus Please come again.

Good by.

Rey

1919

Dear Santa:

It is nearing Christmas and my twin sister and I want tamoshanter for our dolls, Skates and doll cabs apiece, rings, nuts, candy, fruit. remember the Orphans. From your loving friends.

Margaret & Catherine

P.S. Don't forget my cousin, Isabel.

1919

Dear Santa:

I am a little boy five years old If you would please bring me the following things for Christmas I would be thankful. A train and tracks, a live puppy dog, nuts and candy. There will be a lunch on the table for you, and a warm fire so you can warm yorself.

Your little boy.

Vincent

1920

Dear Santa Claus:

Please bring me a mouth Harp, foot ball, and a tool set, some candy, oranges, apples, and chewing gum. I hope the snow isn't too deep for you to come.

James

1920

ROSEDALE, NEW YORK

Dear Santa Claus,

Please bring me a big, big doll with yellow hair and one of those things I have to pull the string and there are colored flowers in and you have to pull the string and all the flowers turn over and you see pretty things in it. And some boots and a sled and two kinds of games. And be sure not to forget me. I live in Rosedale, on Gold Street in the yellow house on Gold street, you have to walk along Ocean Ave. or through the path, but be sure the bull dogs don't bite you.

Muriel

1920

HILLMONT, WYOMING

Dearest Santa Claus:

Christmas will be here very soon and I want to tell you what I want your toy makers to make for me this year. I would thank you very much if you would have your beautiful reindeers bring me some tinker-toys, horn, toolchest, and a seat for my velocipede please that will be all for this time.—O yes, I want some candy too.

I live in a large log house in between to hills. The snow is quite deep here and I am afraid you wont get all over the world this year because your reindeers will be all warn out. But I hope you will be able to go all over all right. It will be all right Santa Clause if you leave the tool chest and the seat for the velocipede at your home this year it will be all right, it might be to big a load for your reindeers. With lots and lots of love to you dear Santa Claus. Age five.

Charles

1920

Dear Old Santa,

As I have been a good girl all year and did just
as my mother, daddy and my teacher asked
me to. I promise to be good for the next year
and not tell any lies to anyone. So I ask you to
please bring me a tricycle, leather school bag,
a baby bumsie doll, and a pair of slippers and
a leather pencil box for Christmas.

Estelle

1920
CHEYENNE, WYOMING

Dear Saint Nick:

I was very much pleased with the presents you gave me last Xmas. And this Xmas I would like to have a pair of roller skates, and a pair of bedroom slippers and don't forget nuts and candy. My stocking will be hanging in the dining room be sure and fill it.

Your loving friend,

Babette